This book is lovingly presented to

For My Child

An Album of Family Memories from Parent to Child

Pictures by
Karen Maloof

Ideals Children's Books • Nashville, Tennessee

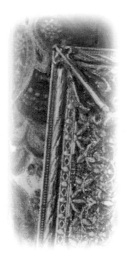

This distinctive volume provides a permanent family record that your child will treasure for a lifetime. Gorgeous hand-tinted photographs adorn pages to which you will add best-loved family photographs and mementos along with important details of family members' lives. There is ample space for information about grandparents, parents, and your child's own history from birth through high school days. A page for special relatives and friends can include members of non-traditional family groupings.

The family record may be created from memories or with gradual additions as your child grows up. A final blank page is provided for recording something special—perhaps a heartfelt wish for your child that you will write upon your presentation of this most meaningful of gifts.

Text copyright © 1994
by Hambleton-Hill Publishing, Inc.
Photographs copyright © 1994 by Karen Maloof

Published by Ideals Children's Books
An imprint of Hambleton-Hill Publishing, Inc.
Nashville, Tennessee 37218

Printed and bound in Mexico.

ISBN 0-8249-8659-8

For My Family-to-Be
—K.M.

Special thanks to:
Eve-Marie Vavagiakis, Ilza Lemisis, B. J. Lerner, Captain Mey's Inn, Bantam Collections, Mom, and my husband.

The display type is set in Benguiat Book.
The text type is set in Galliard.
Color separations were made by Web Tech, Inc., Butler, Wisconsin.
Printed and bound by R. R. Donnelley, Inc.

Our family tree

Child

Brothers and Sisters

Mother   Father

Grandmother   Grandfather   Grandmother   Grandfather

Great-Grandmother   Great-Grandmother   Great-Grandmother   Great-Grandmother

Great-Grandfather   Great-Grandfather   Great-Grandfather   Great-Grandfather

About Mother's parents

Birth name of Grandmother

Date   place

Parents

Brothers and sisters

Hometown

Education

Career

Personality

Birth name of Grandfather

Date   place

Parents

Brothers and sisters

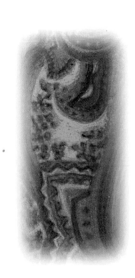

Hometown

Education

Career

Personality

Wedding

Date   place

About Father's parents

Birth name of Grandmother
_____

Date   place
_____

Parents
_____

Brothers and sisters
_____
_____

Hometown
_____

Education
_____

Career
_____

Personality
_____

Birth name of Grandfather
_____

Date   place
_____

Parents
_____

Brothers and sisters
_____
_____

Hometown
_____

Education
_____

Career
_____

Personality
_____

Wedding
_____

Date   place
_____

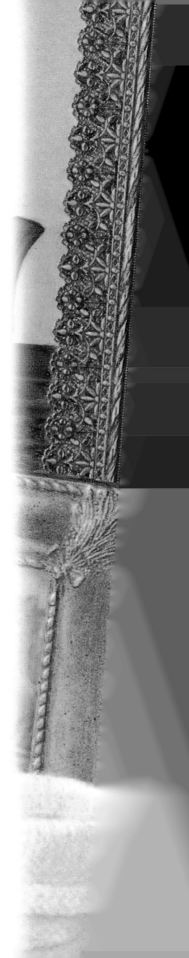

Favorite stories about grandparents

When Mother was born

Birth name
_____

Date _____ place _____

Hair color _____

Eye color _____

Complexion _____

Family resemblances _____
_____
_____
_____

Brothers and sisters _____
_____
_____

Story behind name _____
_____
_____

Personality _____
_____
_____
_____

As a baby _____
_____
_____
_____

When Father was born

Birth name

Date   place

Hair color

Eye color

Complexion

Family resemblances

Brothers and sisters

Story behind name

Personality

As a baby

When Mother was young

Hometown
_____

Hobbies
_____
_____

Friends
_____
_____

Relationships with siblings
_____
_____

Proudest moment
_____
_____

Funniest moment
_____
_____

Ambitions
_____
_____

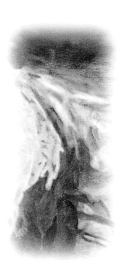

First occupation
_____
_____

When Father was young

Hometown

Hobbies

Friends

Relationships with siblings

Proudest moment

Funniest moment

Ambitions

First occupation

photos or mementos

How Mother and Father met

First met
_____
_____
_____
_____

Impressions
_____
_____
_____

Courtship
_____
_____
_____
_____

Proposal
_____
_____
_____

Engagement
_____
_____
_____

Wedding
_____
Date   place
_____

Special relatives and friends

_____

_____

_____

_____

_____

_____

_____

_____

_____

_____

_____

_____

_____

_____

_____

_____

_____

_____

_____

photos or mementos

You were born

Birth of _____

Date _____ place _____

Height _____ weight _____

Hair color _____

Eye color _____

Complexion _____

Family resemblances _____

_____

_____

Brothers and sisters _____

_____

Story behind name _____

_____

_____

Personality _____

_____

_____

_____

Visitors and gifts _____

_____

_____

photos or mementos

As a baby

Baby's favorites

Foods

Places to go

Songs

Games

Stories

Books

Toys

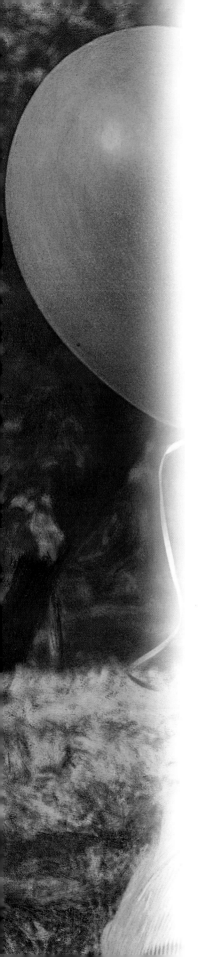

A year of firsts

First smile
_____

_____

First doctor visit
_____

Rolls over
_____

Sits up alone
_____

Sleeps through the night
_____

Crawls
_____

First step
_____

First tooth
_____

First word
_____

First playmate
_____

First mischief
_____

_____

First birthday

Birthday cake

Party attire

Place of party

Family and guests

Gifts

Baby's reaction

Parents' feelings

When you were . . .

One
_____
_____
_____
_____
_____
_____
_____
_____
_____

Two
_____
_____
_____
_____
_____
_____
_____
_____
_____

When you were . . .

Three
_____

_____

_____

_____

_____

_____

_____

Four
_____

_____

_____

_____

_____

_____

Five
_____

_____

_____

_____

_____

_____

First day of school

Date

School

Level

Teacher

The first day

Your reaction

Parents' reactions

Grade school memories

School friends
_____
_____
_____

Best and worst subjects
_____
_____
_____

Report card grades
_____
_____
_____

Favorite school activities
_____
_____
_____

After-school activities
_____
_____
_____

Favorite teachers
_____
_____
_____

photos or mementos

Junior high school years

School friends

_____

_____

_____

Best and worst subjects

_____

_____

_____

Report card grades

_____

_____

Favorite school activities

_____

_____

_____

After-school activities

_____

_____

_____

Favorite teachers

_____

_____

_____

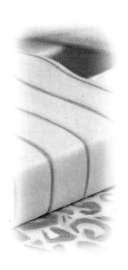

As a young teen

High school memories

School friends
_____
_____
_____

Best and worst subjects
_____
_____
_____

Report card grades
_____
_____

Favorite school activities
_____
_____
_____

After-school activities
_____
_____
_____

Favorite teachers
_____
_____
_____

photos or mementos

High school graduation

Date   place

_____

_____

Family and guests

_____

_____

_____

_____

_____

Gifts

_____

_____

_____

_____

Celebrations

_____

_____

_____

_____

Parents' reactions

_____

_____

_____

_____

_____

photos or mementos

Neighbors and friends

As a child

_____
_____
_____
_____
_____
_____
_____

As a young teen

_____
_____
_____
_____
_____
_____
_____

As a young adult

_____
_____
_____
_____
_____
_____

Family vacations

Holiday memories

photos or mementos

Other stories for you

My wish for you

_____

_____

_____

_____

_____

_____

_____

_____

_____

_____

_____

_____

_____

_____

_____

_____

_____

_____

_____